A Great Light: Finding Meaning at Christmas

Published 2007 by
Veritas Publications
7/8 Lower Abbey Street
Dublin 1
Ireland

Email publications@veritas.ie
Website www.veritas.ie

ISBN 978-1-84730-062-1

All scripture quotations taken from *The New Jerusalem Bible* ©
1985 by Darton, Longman & Todd Ltd and Doubleday &
Company Inc.

A catalogue record for this book is available from the British
Library.

Designed by Lir Mac Cárthaigh
Printed in Ireland by Betaprint, Dublin

Veritas books are printed on paper made from the wood pulp
of managed forests. For every tree felled, at least one tree is
planted, thereby renewing natural resources.

A Great Light

Finding Meaning at Christmas

J.P. Garvey

Contents

Introduction

Look, I bring you news of great joy,
a joy to be shared by the whole people.
                                    Luke 2:10

One of the most exciting and potentially explosive facts about our existence is that not only are we human beings, but we are also spiritual beings with a destiny that will take us far beyond this universe. Perhaps it is something we don't dwell on to any degree, but sometimes the truth of this spiritual reality surfaces in our lives and we feel strange, changed, somehow lifted out of our everyday humanness. We can also feel slightly shy and scared because maybe we are normally so busy being 'human' that this spiritual side of us is pioneer territory. (Think of the experience of falling in love and how it caught us up in the most breathtaking and scary way!)

One of the times spirituality surfaces and resonates in us is during the Christmas period.

The Christmas story has caught the imagination of people young and old for two thousand years. Whether we understand it to be myth or literal truth, or a combination of both – which is the most likely – it still has the power to lead us out of ourselves and our material world into a world of mystery. The story of Christmas is first and foremost a story of joy for the whole of humanity. A new life, a life that is available to everyone, has come into the world.

Tony Flannery, *Waiting in Hope*

There is a prompting inside us to get in touch with this wonder that we sense is about to happen again. The Church provides us with the four weeks of Advent to help us explore where God might be inviting us. The problem is that Christmas is also one of the busiest times of the year when festivities and parties are in full swing. People get subsumed in the clamour of it all – making lists, shopping and hoping finances will cope. In the frantic activity, it can be difficult to find quiet time to think and prepare for the special, sacred time ahead. Failing to set such time aside can lead to feelings of inadequacy. We tell ourselves: 'I'm missing the true meaning of Christmas! I should be more still, I should pray more.' 'Shoulds' and 'oughts' are negative words that usually only lead to negative thoughts and fruitless guilt. Instead of taking on such an unnecessary burden, we might simply say to ourselves: 'What do I want Christmas to mean this year? What actions and activities can help me achieve this?'

Pondering on such simple, yet important questions will inevitably lead us into quiet time with God within us, time that allows us to discern what is really important and meaningful to us, to decide what gives us energy. This will allow all the parts of our lives to become more balanced, more whole, more holy. It will allow us to decide how to celebrate fully the birth of Jesus who came so that all would have life in abundance.

This does not mean that the shopping and partying have to come to a standstill. No, these things are all part of our human need to celebrate, to be people of energy, people full of (God's) spirit. But in the midst of the festivities, we can still wait, still listen and allow God to speak. This is possible but not easy. Waiting runs contrary to our whole cultural push and listening means being silent at times – and that too is not a modern phenomenon. If we try to be aware that the four-week period leading up to Christmas is really geared to help us trust in our own potential for greatness, to dig a little deeper into our understanding of why Christ wanted to live among us, we will find a sense of calm and wonder which will feed into everything we do at this time. Patrick Kavanagh says it so much more beautifully:

> We have tested and tasted too much lover
> through a chink too wide there comes in
> no wonder
> but here in this Advent darkened room
> where the dry black bread and sugarless
> tea
> of penance will charm back the luxury
> of a child's soul, we'll return to Doom
> the knowledge we stole and could not
> use.
>
> 'Advent'

Kavanagh was deeply aware of the need to nourish our spiritual selves – to be merely human is not enough. We have a yearning, a 'wish' inside us that is insatiable. Often, our experience is that when we realise a hoped-for wish we are not completely satisfied – the 'wish' is still there! We seem to be ever-searching for something to fill the gap. St Augustine came to know that there is a space inside us that none but God can fill: 'You have made us for yourself, O God, and our hearts are restless until they rest in you.'

Advent gives us a time to ease our restlessness, to wait with God in silence, expectation and hope. In a sense, there will always be an Advent in our lives, but at Christmas it reaches new heights. God is coming again and we have new opportunity to be the people we want to be.

✛ A TIME OF TOGETHERNESS

At Christmas, much focus is placed on families and on being together in harmony. And it is true that, for many, there are blessings to be found in returning to the familiar rhythm of the family Christmas, when adults can become wide-eyed children again, sharing in the wonder of the angels through the singing of carols, reliving the magic of Santa as old friends are greeted, presents are exchanged and meals are prepared and shared.

The trouble is, the soft glow of such a gathering is not the experience of all and even in the most functional of families, attempts to create Christmas cheer can test the gentlest of souls. Furthermore, not everyone lives in a family and being alone at this time of year can be miserable. If you have lost a partner or a loved one then the very memory of past happy times can make this time of year particularly difficult.

Does God really understand how difficult it can be for us? How sometimes people come to dread Christmas? Helmut Thielicke put it like this:

> Jesus Christ did not remain at the bare headquarters in heaven, receiving reports of the world's suffering from below and shouting a few encouraging words to us from a safe distance. No, he left the

headquarters and came down to us in the front-line trenches, right down to where we live and worry about what the Bolsheviks may do, where we contend with our anxieties and the feeling of emptiness and futility, where we sin and suffer guilt, and where we must finally die. There is nothing he did not endure with us. He understands everything.

We can take heart from the promise of our opening scripture text: that God wants to be involved with us, that he is at work in our lives, that he wants us to experience joy. He is not a God that has favourites, but he showers his gifts on all those who wish them.

I suspect a common feature in all our lives which can prove an obstacle to believing that God is at work in us is a nagging sense of inadequacy that leads us almost instinctively to believe that this could not be happening to us – 'I'm not good enough, not holy enough – I don't pray properly and I rarely go to Mass'. But it wasn't just because of the goodness of Mary that God worked such wonders for her. It was because the power of God came and rested on her. In the same way, it is the power of God resting on us that brings him to life in us. When in doubt about one's innate goodness and value, it is worth remembering the assurance of the book of Genesis: 'Let us make man in our own image, in the likeness of ourselves ... God saw all he had made, and indeed it was very good' (1:26, 31).

The amazing truth is that God has put himself in a position where he needs us – to be his voice, his hands, his feet; to carry him to places he cannot go without us. Jesus gave us a mission to 'go out to the whole world; proclaim the Good News to all creation (Mark 16:15). In so doing, he made us integral to God's plan. In and through our own brokenness, we can look around us and heal wounds, mend relationships, feed the hungry and be gospel (which means good news) to those around us. We can cooperate with God and Christmas gives us a renewed chance to listen to what he might be saying to us, a time to be willing to let him break through and take us to a deeper, happier life.

We must open that door to taste the good things God wants to share with us. The following chapters will help us to do this during the hectic weeks leading up to Christmas. We will take a fresh look at problems we all have when it comes to issues such as finances, present buying and family relations, and examine how we can view Christmas time as an opportunity to approach these in new ways.

✝ PRAYER

Lord, during this Christmas season, help us to give ourselves the gift of enough time; enough time to laugh and cry, to work and play, to run and be still. Teach us that the unreflected life can lead us to places that we would not choose to be. Help us to heed to words of Jesus 'to come away and rest awhile' so that we may then rise and go many miles in the direction that is life-giving for us and for those we love.

Families at Christmas

*His mother Mary was betrothed to Joseph,
but before they came to live together she was
found to be with child through the Holy Spirit.
Her husband Joseph, being a man of honour
and wanting to spare her publicly, decided to
divorce her informally. He had made up his
mind to do this when the angel of the Lord
appeared to him in a dream and said, 'Joseph,
son of David, do not be afraid to take Mary
home as your wife, because she has conceived
what is in her by the Holy Spirit'.*

Matthew 1:18-21

In the Ireland of the forties and fifties the notion of family was a sacred chalice made up of husband/wife and approximately six kids. This ideal was accepted by church and state as the norm. State divorce did not exist, separations were rare and many who suffered in ill-suited relationships saw little alternative but to remain trapped and constrained by societal pressures and expectations.

The supports underpinning this system would inevitably crack as increasing numbers stepped away from prisons of abuse and misery and chose alternative paths. And as more and more people questioned the sanity of remaining in deeply unhappy marriages, the Catholic Church under Vatican II decided that it was time for the whole Church to step aside and look at itself and how it was serving the People of God. Windows in many areas of

Church life that had remained shut tight for centuries were pushed open and a new spirit of openness and reflection was ushered in.

Looking at the concept of family in this country some forty years later we must be prepared to see it in a much broader way. A definition for today's family could be 'a loving situation in which children are nurtured and reared'. This is an inclusive definition that opens it arms to the different situations in which children are brought up. What happened at the nativity was the essence of inclusivity: Jesus was born for everyone who exists – no one was excluded.

All families are made up of imperfect people who make mistakes. Even the happiest-looking families can be hiding great pain and distress. The circumstances of the birth of Jesus were hardly idyllic. By unpacking the nativity story we can see the wretched circumstances in which they found themselves: Mary young, unmarried and pregnant, Joseph knowing he was not the father, had decided to divorce her quietly. In doing so, he was acting honourably. The norms of his culture would have allowed, indeed expected him to expose her to public ridicule and humiliation. He then had a huge change of heart (this must have taken much soul-searching despite the way it is summarily treated in the gospel account). According to the Lucan narrative, Mary then disappeared for three months, going to see her cousin Elizabeth, probably leaving Joseph very confused and uncertain. Some time after her return, with Mary heavily pregnant, they undertook an arduous journey, received very little welcome, had a less than ideal birth experience and, as Herod ordered the execution of all the male babies under two years old, they were forced to become political refugees in a country that had long oppressed their people. How must they have felt in this situation of terror and uncertainty – which only a short time before was being heralded as a time of unprecedented joy? And yet, this is part of the paradox, the mystery of Christmas – that it is in the midst of the turmoil (and not only in its absence) that joy can be found if we know how to recognise it.

So let's not be too hard on ourselves; let's simply believe that the little child in Bethlehem was born for us – and this makes everything possible.

+ PLANNING FOR CHRISTMAS AS A FAMILY

So how does your family square up for Christmas? What would it take for you and your family to enjoy a happy and peaceful Christmas? It is a well-known fact that events that are planned have a greater chance of being successful: families that set goals are more likely to get what they want. The people most likely to set these goals are the guardians – parents, grandparents etc. – and, as the children mature, they should be also be involved. Here are some tips:

- Make a list of all the things that need to get done. Prioritise, even strike some items off the list – are they all absolutely necessary?

- Plan rest time into Christmas day so that you have time to step back and appreciate the festivities.

- Get your Christmas cards organised and posted early in the winter – around

October/November time. Make a list of all the people you need to send a card to – this will allow you to work out how many cards you need to get as well as helping you to keep track of who you've sent cards to. If you don't have time to go shopping for Christmas cards, why not consider sending e-cards, especially to some of your overseas friends and family?

• Begin thinking about and shopping for Christmas presents early so that you're not panicking at the last minute, desperately buying gifts for people you're not even sure they will like. If you hate shopping in the city or in busy shopping centres, try shopping online and get all your gifts delivered straight to your door – just make sure you place your orders before the last Christmas post.

• Whatever you are planning to cook for Christmas, preparation is the key. Prepare as much of the food as possible on Christmas Eve – peel and soak some of the vegetables, boil the ham so it's ready for roasting etc. – so you have less to do on the big day. Remember to find out in advance if any of your dinner guests have special dietary requirements (vegetarian, coeliac etc.). You could also consider avoiding cooking all together and eating out! If you're planning on doing this, make sure you book a few months in advance to avoid disappointment.

• In many families, there always seems to be someone who likes to argue and complain. If you have someone like this spending Christmas Day with you, plan in advance what topics are likely to set this person off on a rant and what topics are more likely to lead to pleasant conversation – stick to the latter! If this is impossible, prepare yourself and remember to try to stay calm and maybe even remove yourself from these situations. If you find that something like alcohol fuels these situations then it maybe best to either limit the alcohol available or just avoid it all together.

- Arrange a time around Christmas – perhaps in the days following Christmas Day – to spend with family members or friends that you enjoy being with but you may be too busy for at other times. Plan for special time to spend with your children and partner too, especially if the lead-up to Christmas promises to be chaotic.

- As we will discuss later on, families are important for teenagers – even if they sometimes appear like they would rather spend time with anyone else! Find a compromise – maybe they could spend some time with the family and some time with their friends.

✚ COUNTING THE COST

Some of the biggest problems families face are financial. When these are not tackled properly, families can find themselves stretching their money too thin, borrowing too much and landing themselves in real trouble. Coming up to Christmas, worries about money can put great pressure on people. The average Irish household is due to spend €1,300 this Christmas, which is nearly double that of our European counterparts. The Financial Regulator has warned consumers that a loan is 'not just for Christmas'. The regulator's Consumer Director, Mary O'Dea has said: 'Borrowing money at this time of year may be the only way for some people to meet Christmas expenses. However, once Christmas is over, the money is spent and you will have to make repayments long after the Christmas holiday'. Remember, Jesus, Mary and Joseph offered nothing but themselves – but what an offering. We must never devalue what a gift each of us can be to others. It is through each one of us that God reaches out to the world.

Well in advance of Christmas, decide on a budget, with your partner or family if appropriate. Take everything into consideration – write it all down and look at it objectively: do you really need everything on the list? Don't fall into the trap of believing that you have to spend a lot of money to enjoy Christmas Day.

In today's time-poor society, the gift of your time can be precious. Consider giving your friend with the out-of-control garden the gift of your time every Saturday afternoon for the next month; babysitting for your friends who have a young baby and who are dying to have a night out together; visiting your elderly neighbour in the nursing home every second Sunday.

If you decide to go this route, don't be embarrassed if someone unexpectedly gives you a very expensive gift in return. Don't feel as though you have to match the cost of this gift in order to be worthy of receiving it. Remind yourself that this person chose to give this present to you as a symbol of their affection. Can you accept it graciously in the spirit of how it was given or are you too worried of how you might appear to a critical eye? It is part of the Christian tradition to accept gifts without asking and to receive more than we could ever repay: we could never dream of repaying God for the gift of his Son and life everlasting.

✝ TEACHING CHILDREN THE MEANING OF CHRISTMAS

When it comes to your children, remember that it is your responsibility to teach them values, to teach them that having lots of material things won't make them happy, that money is not the measure of satisfaction.

If you feel pressured by media advertisements to spend more than you can afford, talk with your children about what Christmas really means to you and your family, and what is really important. Teach your children that real happiness is found elsewhere. Talk to them about the birth of Jesus and what you believe is the important message of Christmas. Make use of the variety of children's books which draw out the meaning of the birth of Jesus. Revisit the classics like Charles Dickens' *A Christmas Carol* to underline your message in an enjoyable way.

In consultation with your partner or fellow guardian, get over the fear of discussing money with children. To some degree, and from an appropriate age, your kids need to be educated about reality. Let your children know that you simply cannot afford all the expensive toys they see advertised on TV. Otherwise the retail trade will bleed you dry of all your money – as well as money that isn't even yours! And being financially stressed in the New Year is a recipe for tension and arguments.

Think about alternative presents that your children could give their friends and family. How about baking Christmas cookies or making candles together? Granny would be delighted to receive a hand-made present from her favourite grandchild! Once they are of a certain age, why not introduce your children to the notion of charity and justice. Contact Trócaire, St Vincent de Paul, Bóthar or Focus and see how you and your children could lend a hand to those less fortunate – at Christmas time and perhaps beyond. I invite you to look again at the Introduction to this book and recall what the four-week period of Advent can do for us, why Christ wanted to come among us. It will help you focus on that deep peace that Christmas offers.

✝ WHEN TENSIONS ERUPT

We may earnestly strive for the perfect Christmas, putting sensible plans in place, budgeting and so on, yet despite our best efforts disagreements and quarrels break out and in no time all the good intentions and Christmas ideals seem to lie broken at our feet and cold hostility creeps in.

Try to bounce back. Think about the kind of Christmas you really want for yourself and your family and realise that the way to get this is not through hostility and a frosty atmosphere. Quite often, a quick apology is needed and perhaps another affirmation to try to keep the peace and appreciate all that we are blessed with at Christmas. Remember the real story of the nativity – that it was in the midst of turmoil and uncertainty that real happiness and hope were to be found.

✝ TIPS

• Remember that no family is perfect. Part of the mystery of Christmas is that hope and joy can be found in chaos and turmoil.

- Plan for the kind of Christmas you want – events that are planned are far more likely to be successful.

- Set a budget and stick to it!

- Teach your children that there is more to Christmas than the giving of presents. Talk to them about the birth of Jesus and what you believe is the real meaning of Christmas.

- If tensions erupt, deal with them swiftly so that they don't fester and ruin the entire day.

✛ PRAYER

Christmas offers us the chance to be
at our best, to let the clouds of anger
or resentment roll away and let the
song of the angels be heard. With
mindful planning, our Christmas
traditions – the family gatherings, the
presents and the celebrations – can all
bear witness to the fact that God is
close to us and that we are able to
create relationships of inclusion,
equality, justice and love. Help us
Lord, to be just, forgiving and loving
in all that we do this Christmas.

Estranged at Christmas

The spirit of the Lord is on me
for he has anointed me
to bring the good news to the afflicted.
He has sent me
to proclaim liberty to captives,
sight to the blind,
to let the oppressed go free,
to proclaim a year of favour
from the Lord.

Luke 4:18-19

We know that many relationships break down. We know what pain and suffering people experience and the guilt that people often feel because they couldn't make things work. In 'Hedges Freaked with Snow', the poet Robert Graves paints a very calm and reasoned picture of the break-up of a relationship:

> No argument, no anger, no remorse,
> no dividing of blame.
> There was poison in the cup – why
> should we ask from whose hand it came?

Perhaps this smacks of heroic acceptance and self-control, but in truth we are only human and despite our best efforts things do collapse. Being human necessarily entails a measure of brokenness. If we could accept this truth, perhaps anger, blame and bitterness could be minimised, like in the poem.

The scripture passage above strongly asserts that it was for the broken-hearted, those who experience failure, that Christ came on earth. At the beginning of his public ministry, Jesus proclaimed clearly that his mission was to be on the side of the poor and the downtrodden. It is true that in heightened emotional states God's healing power might not easily come to mind, but perhaps at this time of year we could pause and reflect on all the grace that this season is reminding us of: the grace of God's unconditional love, the message of Isaiah that we are carved on the palms of God's hands (49), that in our brokenness and flawed humanity we are loved beyond measure and that nothing can separate us from the love of God (Romans 8:38-39). Accepting such assurances can help us in the midst of the anguish of separation, insofar as is possible, to find the strength to plan for fair and equitable arrangements for the celebrations of the season.

✛ WHERE WILL THE CHILDREN SPEND CHRISTMAS DAY?

All of this is not to deny that when parents in a family live separately, Christmas can be particularly challenging. Do you all get together for the day? Do the children have two Christmas dinners? Do you alternate each year? There is no set formula of rules for how it should be. The important thing is to create Christmas experiences that children can enjoy with all members of their families.

For many separated parents, organising Christmas is just another part of their ongoing strategy for cooperating around their children's care and needs. They are used to putting their children first during the year and Christmas is just one more time when they do this.

Involving children in some discussions about Christmas arrangements may be a really good idea. However, it is important that they don't feel they are being asked to choose between their parents, or to feel responsible for a parent who may be left to spend Christmas without them. So the timing of visits and the length of stay might be more useful discussions than questions such as, 'Who do you want to spend Christmas with this year?'

If you are on friendly terms with your ex, coming to an amicable agreement about where the children will spend the special days of Christmas, i.e. Christmas Eve and Christmas Day – with Mum, with Dad, with both together for just these two days or with grandparents – might not be too difficult. But what if the separation is recent and the hurt is raw? What if you can't bear the sight and sound of your ex? What if they already have a new partner? How will you cope and look after the children? In situations like these, it is OK to admit that you're out of your depth, that you can't handle the emotional challenge on your own. Reach out – to family, close friends or a counsellor. Consider appointing a third, impartial person to negotiate between you and your ex. Talk to organisations such as ACCORD, Relate or Gingerbread who can offer support and advice (see end of book for contact details).

If you will be spending Christmas Day with your children, bear in mind that your children may be missing your ex and may want to talk to them or talk about them. Allow them to do this and try to hide whatever hurt this might cause you. Think what a shift in their world this new change is. They have lived with you both for years and love you both hugely. It is very hard for them to understand the adult situation they are part of. If you are able, encourage the children to phone your ex, make a card for them during the day or save them some Christmas cake. It is important that they feel able to express their excitement and love towards their parent without angering you.

Avoid criticising your ex in front of your children – it makes children most uncomfortable and they may resent you for it in the future. Remember that your children are, genetically, half you, half your ex, so to criticise your ex is to inadvertently criticise them. Children must never be made to feel responsible for the breakdown of the relationship; never enter into the blaming syndrome – leave it aside and concentrate on making these days happy for the children.

If you will not be spending Christmas Day with the children, try to stay upbeat in front of them. Let them know that you'll be visiting friends and/or family so they won't worry about you being lonely. If you're planning on taking part in some charity activity, let them know all about it – they might want to join you next year. However, make it clear that you will miss them and that you're looking forward to meeting up with them afterwards. Plan a few special days after Christmas and express your excitement at getting to celebrate Christmas twice.

For all of us – adults and children – Christmas traditions are so important. Separation will bring changes and many of these traditions risk being lost. Children will miss them. Consider talking to them about this – ask them if they're worried about Christmas, if they're sad that things might not be the way they used to be. Find out if there are any particular traditions or rituals that they really love and see if you can keep these going. All traditions have a beginning, so consider starting some new ones. If you won't be with the children on Christmas Day, in the weeks/days preceding Christmas maybe get them to help you make the Christmas pudding or mince pies, ask them to sign the Christmas cards or hang up some new decorations.

You might also consider starting some new traditions just for yourself: make time for visiting close friends; have some time to yourself to relax and unwind; take part in a fun run for charity. Doing your best to embrace change and enjoy your life is a great example to give to your children.

+ MIND YOURSELF

Children are very perceptive. They pick up on even slight mood changes, particularly in those they love and depend on – such as their parents. They will be especially sensitive during the time of a separation. You can't hide the pain completely from them – nor should you. It is okay for children to know that their parents are human and have emotions too. When they are of an appropriate age, let them know that you are going through a tough time – that sometimes you feel sad. It is good for them to feel that they have your confidence – that you value them and respect them enough to let them into your world. Make sure, however, that you stress how much you love them and how they bring you such joy. Let them know that they are not responsible for your moods – that if you appear grumpy it's not because of anything they have done.

Children are prone to feeling guilty during their parents' separation, so it is important that they don't interpret your hurt as anger towards them. Consider having a code word – something the children can say to you when they see you are sad or angry and are worried you are cross at them. This word should give you a little jolt – bring you out of yourself and alert you to their anxiety.

Without being intrusive, give the children a chance to express how they are feeling – have mini-checks on their emotions. Bear in mind, however, that children often find it very hard to express what they are feeling – they may not understand the sadness or the anger inside them or be able to find the words to describe what they feel. Therefore, while rules are still important and children should not be allowed to get away with being overly rude or physically violent, try to make allowances for distant or sullen moods.

During a separation, one or both of the parents may find that they are spending a lot of time with the children and are very focused on them and their needs. However, it is crucial that you make sure that you have appropriate adult support. Allow yourself time with a family member, close friend or counsellor. Vent and express your anger, hurt, sadness, fear – let it out and talk about it. Take responsibility for your negative feelings and begin to figure out how you are going to get beyond them.

✚ REMEMBER YOUR BUDGET

Finances are often hit hard with a break-up before Christmas. It is important not to overdo the children's presents in an attempt to make them feel better about the upheaval in their home life. If possible, agree in advance with your ex about who will get what presents. Try not to compete with each other for the best present. Your children will feel happier getting something from both of you which is given in a genuine loving spirit.

Christmas memories are so important to children creating an environment where they can feel safe and secure is vital. But don't beat yourself up worrying about how you might be ruining their memories. Just concentrate on making the most of what you have and do your best to create a safe and loving Christmas this year and into the future.

✛ FAMILY FEUDS

What of estranged families – brothers and sisters that haven't spoken in years, mothers and daughters that can't be in the same room as each other? Christmas is a time when this hurt weighs heavier on the heart and a part of us longs for reconciliation. This can be very difficult as silence and resentment may have prevailed for years.

If there is someone you and your family are holding resentment towards, consider if you can bring yourself towards forgiveness. It may not be realistic or possible for you to welcome them back with open arms – things rarely change overnight – but small efforts can add up to eventual peace and healing. Talk to other members of your family or a trusted mutual friend and see if they might be able to mediate.

If there is serious dispute between you and another family member, ask yourself if it might be time to put whatever hurt you hold aside. Try to remember what this person was like before the hurt began; remember what you valued in them. Consider that these positive characteristics are more than likely still within this person – can you bring yourself to see them again? Ask yourself if you could survive letting your guard down and allowing this person to come a little closer. In their book, *Design for Wholeness: Dealing With Anger, Learning to Forgive, Building Self Esteem*, the authors, Loughlan Sofied, Carroll Juliano and Rosine Hammett write:

> A distinguishing mark of Christians should be the presence of forgiveness and the willingness to seek reconciliation, not the absence of anger and conflict in their lives. The concept of willingness to seek reconciliation cannot be overlooked for in some situations reconciliation will not be possible ... the choice to let go of resentment is to choose life. It is holding on to anger and resentment that ultimately

dulls the life within us. The choice to forgive often brings with it a feeling of relief, a freedom of spirit and renewed life. It is often the one who forgives rather than the person who is forgiven who receives the greater benefit.

(p. 56)

What if you have been shunned by a family member(s)? Do you understand why? Have you spent years trying to make amends for a mistake you made some time ago? This is a very difficult situation and there is no, one easy solution. Only you can decide if it's worth trying again and whether you feel there may be room again in the heart of your family. If so, remember that even if you are met with a positive response, it is unrealistic to expect all hurt to evaporate instantly: 'the mind can accept the slow process of dissipation of anger long before the heart is comfortable with this reality' (ibid, p. 61).

If you feel your attempts to reconcile will inevitably be rejected, then do not give up on the decision to forgive: 'to forgive is an act of compassion toward oneself ... forgiveness is primarily an act of the will and an inner decision to divest oneself of self-destructive emotions' (ibid, pp. 61–2).

Try to be patient and compassionate and open to the possibility of eventual movement in others. Surround yourself with people who love you for who you are now. Accept that you cannot change people. Allow yourself forgiveness and the opportunity to move on and leave the pain behind. Perhaps in time those with whom you are now estranged may follow.

✛ TIPS

- Decide where the children will spend Christmas – ask for the help of an impartial third party, if necessary.

- Allow your children to talk about your ex without making them feel they have done something wrong.

- If you will not be with the children on Christmas Day, make plans and new traditions for yourself and the children in the subsequent days of the season.

- To a certain degree, let your children know if you are feeling sad or upset.

- Reassure your children that none of this is their fault.

- Allow them to express their own hurt.

- Don't forget to set a budget and stick to it!

- If you are estranged from family members, allow forgiveness to begin to grow in your heart.

✚ PRAYER

When the day is long, the hurt immense and the disappointments of life threaten to overwhelm me, help me to trust that you hold me in the palm of your hand and that you will guide my heart in the ways of your love so that this Christmas can open new paths of peace and hope which hold the promise of compassion and forgiveness.

Young Adults
at Christmas

*You have already been told what is right
and what Yahweh wants of you.
Only this, to do what is right,
to love loyalty
and to walk humbly with your God.*

Micah 6:8

The presence of young children in the family circle at Christmas adds an extra dimension to everyone's enjoyment of the day. To see their wide-eyed excitement and happiness allows us to relive those times when we were full of joy and without a worry or care. They live in a world of very simple faith and joy and have no problem accepting the biblical account of Christ's birth in Bethlehem. Those of us who have watched children perform in nativity plays in school will have envied their total identification with what was unfolding. Indeed, it helps us reconnect with the wonder and magic of the Christmas story, touching us with its innocence and majesty. Young children add a very special yeast to those few days of Christmas.

As they grow up and bump into life head-on, influenced by their peers and not wanting to seem so innocent, so beguiled, they become more cautious and questioning, more self-reliant. A lot of the simple magic is reluctantly left behind. Sometimes the child would really love to enter again into the magic, but on the other hand is firmly held back by the influence of peers and their fears and doubts. They feel they are required to grow up, but step cautiously into such territory.

✛ CHANGING TRADITIONS

Then come the teenage years, with all their attendant hormonal fluxes, demands for greater freedom, rising independence. Teenagers tend to be emotionally volatile and hypersensitive, and everything about Christmas exacerbates this. Usually the Christmas home programme remains much as it always was, but young people begin to suffer from Christmas cabin-fever. Of course, they love their families, but the growing importance of a wider social life begins to compete. They start to feel resentful of having to spend the entire day indoors, playing charades, card games, happy families, when they would much rather be out socialising with friends. Many teenagers are frustrated with the lack of control they exert over their own lives, and the tensions of Christmas tend to heighten this feeling. Maybe now is the time to create new ways of spending those few very important Christmas days.

Now that children have become young adults, they should be consulted as to what might be changed; and even if this does not produce significant alterations, at least it would have been discussed and opportunities created for honest dialogue. For example, must it still be obligatory for the whole family to go to Midnight Mass? Must Christmas dinner be timed inflexibly for 2.30 p.m.? Must relatives be visited on Christmas morning, when maybe some people might be happier to rest at home? Could it be agreed that, say, an hour after dinner young people could be free to visit their friends?

Families are notorious for creating traditions that become cast in stone after many years and take on the character of myth: 'We always have a perfect Christmas day'; 'Everyone must be happy on Christmas day'; 'We must stay together on this day or people will be upset.' The reality is often very different, with many families struggling through the day, hoping to get by without an argument, muttering at the end of it, 'Thank God that's over for another year'. Real dialogue can prevent this happening in your family this Christmas; after all, we are celebrating the birth of Christ – the king of inclusivity! It does seem wrong not to make sure that each member of the family feels that it is their own celebration. Looking at it this way, there is quite an obligation on everyone to be other-centred. Everyone should have the chance to vote on how the day should be spent.

If a row or a sulk does end up happening, it is important to deal with it straight away, not to let it fester for the entire day. Try to discuss what is seen to be the problem and to formulate a compromise that everyone is happy with. This could be the agreement that the teenager can go out after dinner to meet up with friends, or can call their boyfriend or girlfriend after the relatives have gone home.

A family Christmas should be a kind of infrastructure through which the miracle of the Incarnation can be made present to each member of the family. It must remain open and inclusive – parents must try to ensure that they don't choke the spontaneous creativity that this huge event brings into our lives. No domination, no control tactics, no binding people to traditions that no longer make for happiness. If you have read the amazing book *Amongst Women*, by John McGahern, you will know what I mean. The main character – the father, Moran – is a bully and a control freak. Christmas day was a painful event for all:

> As always, it was a very long day to get through. Moran ate alone in front of the big sideboard mirror, waited on apprehensively by the girls. After he had eaten they had their own dinner at the side table. Afterwards the radio was played. The Rosary was said. The pack of cards was taken out. Everybody made for their beds early. It was a gladness to slip down into the sheets knowing the day had ended.

How awful would it be to realise that any member of your family couldn't wait for Christmas day to end!

For the older, married or engaged children in a family, other constraints are often felt. Again, there is the feeling that to depart from the family home is somehow breaking the traditions of Christmas, ruining the day for other members. However, as with many other things in life, as one gets older within the family circle, one finds that change is not only necessary, it is inevitable. Trying to cling on to the traditions of old is often a futile exercise. In such instances, it must be made acceptable to leave the family home and spend time with other loved ones. Indeed, it might often be the case that Mum and Dad might appreciate the evening to themselves – to reminisce, to relax, to enjoy each other's company – and would prefer an empty house for a couple of hours. Or indeed, maybe both parents would really love to go away for the Christmas season – to a hotel, abroad even – but feel unable to make such a suggestion at the risk of seeming selfish.

What all such suggestions lead us back to is the importance of open and honest dialogue.

It is worthless trying to desperately hold on to the way things were, or the way we imagined things to be when we were young. This only leads to rows and resentment on Christmas day. How about making new traditions, new memories?

Regarding members of the family who have spouses, which set of parents to visit, who to have dinner with, who to invite over, can often prove most problematic. This is an unnecessary stress, deriving again from constraints imposed on families designed to maintain the traditions of Christmas. Again, what must be realised is that as time moves on, situations change, traditions change. It can often be quite an inconvenience trying to fit two sets of in-laws into the day. Even more so, should families live quite a distance apart, deciding which family to spend the few days with can prove challenging and even divisive. Visiting each of the sets on alternating years can often be the way to go, but this again precludes new families from spending any time in their own home on Christmas Day. In such instances, finances might decide; however, it might also be an idea to suggest that those wishing to are more than welcome to visit you. In such a case, a new tradition is borne out of familial necessity.

If you are visiting your in-laws for the first time this Christmas Day, keep in mind that it will probably be different to what you are used to. They may have different traditions: a different time for the meal; they may go to mass, or not; there may be a big gathering with lots of small children running around the place; there may be none at all. In such an instance, sit back and relax. You have no control over what happens nor how it happens. Perhaps, in advance, it might be a good idea to get a run-down from your partner of what might be expected.

The key yet again to avoiding such issues is open and honest dialogue, with just a bit of understanding and consideration. Family discussions a month or two in advance can put everyone on the same page and reduce the element of surprise in the days coming up to Christmas.

In summary, family traditions can often spell family rows. People feel obliged to partake and revel in the homestead atmosphere, and all forced revelry often results in sulky teenagers and disgruntled adults. Inter-family dialogue is of utmost importance. Finding out what people want and would enjoy is the safest route to a harmonious house at Christmas. A little bit of give and take, consideration for the wants of others, and a calm demeanour all help towards the enjoyment of Christmas and of each other.

+ TIPS FOR TEENS

- Discuss with the family what it is everyone wants to do this Christmas. Take into account all opinions and organise accordingly. Have this discussion before Christmas, giving teenagers a say in what happens.

- Don't expect teenagers to want to stay at home the entire day. And don't separate boyfriends and girlfriends for too long.

- Plan for things to do after the food and present-opening. Get out games that appeal to all ages, make a video or take photos on a mobile, or get the guitars out. But be flexible and don't force games on the family.

- Involve them in tasks of their choosing: decorating the table, making an alternative to Christmas pudding, putting together a compilation of festive music.

- If Christmas Day is full of dutiful visits a teenager won't enjoy much, let them choose a family outing immediately before or after.

✛ TIPS FOR NEW FAMILIES

- Accept change as not only being necessary, but inevitable. Try to open out into new possibilities for enjoying Christmas.

- Understand that not everyone celebrates the holiday season the way you might be used to. Every family has its own way of passing the day, be that with a house full of children or with none at all. Enjoy the day for what it is.

• Establish new traditions: open your own house up to your in-laws, and make it possible for them to visit you. In this way, family is included, but the foundations are laid for future Christmas rituals.

✝ PRAYER

As Christmas time approaches, help me to heed the words of the prophet Micah and remember that all I am asked to do is to be just and loving in my relationships. Let my family teach me: help me listen more and speak less, to let go of my pre-conceptions of how things ought to be. In so doing, my actions will help 'Prepare a way for the Lord' (Luke 3:4) who came so all would know love and acceptance.

Lonely at
Christmas

If only my misery could be weighed,
and all my ills put on the scales!
But they outweigh the sands of the seas:
What wonder then if my words are wild?
                                              Job 6:2-3

To a greater or lesser degree most of us have been touched by the reality of loneliness, even for short spaces of time. Loneliness can be experienced even when one is in the midst of a great group of people, at work or in the home. But, for most it often passes again once we come to realise the love and support others have for us. For some, however, these spaces lengthen and become darker and more consuming. It seems that there is no way to shake free from the terrible feeling of aloneness. Our opening passage from the book of Job reminds us of the desolation that so many endure. This of course is especially pronounced at the time of year that promotes the reunion of families maybe distanced by geography or time, and the excitement and exuberance of parties, presents and indulgence.

Those who have never felt this entrapment and utter loneliness find it very difficult to empathise with how frightening it can be. The poet Gerard Manley Hopkins described it thus:

> No worst, there is none. Pitched past pitch of grief,
> More pangs will, schooled at forepangs, wilder wring.
> Comforter, where, where is your comforting?
> Mary, mother of us, where is your relief?

Hopkins was a Jesuit priest, living in community with others and yet prey to near despair. He goes on to describe what a terrifying place the mind can become. 'Oh the mind, mind has mountains;/Cliffs of fall frightful, no man fathomed.' Hopkins wrote three sonnets (called 'The Terrible Sonnets'), all trying to describe the awfulness of aloneness, the despair of guilt and the burden of depression. Even the mere reading of them makes you thank God that you have never been drawn down to such depths. Robert

Frost, the American poet, could associate with such feelings:

> I have been acquainted all the night
> I have walked out in vain – and back in rain
> I have outwalked the furthest city light ...

People live with varying degrees of loneliness – even those who seem the brightest and most social often wrestle with this fear of aloneness. For many of us, these feelings don't often hit us because we have people around us whom we love and who love us; but what happens when, for whatever reason, those we lean on for love and compassion are taken away? The memory of a loved one now gone; of a chance for love passed up; family far away; siblings estranged: there are any number of reasons people find themselves passing the Christmas season alone. We wrap ourselves up and withdraw from the world. People will be kind and helpful and as understanding as they can be, but we feel so alone. How does the Christmas Child break through the barriers we erect?

The time of announced salvation for all must somehow reach out to those in pain, and we must try in our way to mediate this grace through our thoughtfulness, sensitivity and respect for where the lonely are in their life journeys. To hark back to the beginning of the book, we pointed out that Jesus came principally for the marginalised, the suffering and the weak among mankind. His aim and his mission was wide open to those on the edge of society, for those who felt they had no one to confide in, no one to love or be loved by. And indeed, Jesus constantly showed his empathy for such people on the margins; did he not cry out to his Father before he died: 'My God, my God, why have you forsaken me?' Did he not feel utterly alone? Even during his thirty-three years on earth, was he ever able to confide in anyone the huge burden he carried? Remember when he was separated from his parents in the temple. His reply to Mary when she asked where he was: 'Did you not know I must be in my Father's house?' No, Mary did not know. And as his business increased on earth, he felt increasingly alone. If, as Thomas Wolfe said, 'Loneliness is and always has been the central and inevitable experience of every man', how much more can this have been true for Christ.

All this can be of scant comfort to those in the throes of depression and loneliness at a time of festive cheer, celebration and togetherness. However, from Christ there is infinite love and comfort – however he works through us! We are his understanding, his compassion, his love. God made man feels the loneliness that we feel, the isolation and the anguish, because he felt these emotions during his time amongst us. We need faith and hope in huge measure – believing that when we are most alone, most in the pain of aloneness, God is closest. It is God's essential mission – to rescue us from ourselves, to offer us healing: 'Come to me, all you who labour and are overburdened, and I will give you rest.' (Matthew 11:28) Christ spent his three public years reaching out to people, curing, healing, comforting and loving. He would hold us in the palm of his hand if we would let him. It is this we should remember during the period of Advent. We expectantly await the arrival of Jesus, our Saviour and Redeemer, the one who will comfort us in our times of distress, loneliness and isolation. We await him as he awaits our turning to him in such abandoned times. We are lucky if our faith has a strong foundation, if we can feel like the psalmist, 'Even were I to walk in a ravine as dark as death I shoud fear no danger, for you are at my side' (Psalms 23:4), and yes, of course, God's grace and help are such an essential part of Advent.

A decision is needed to move out of our pain shelter. Dag Hammarskjöld, the former UN Secretary General, said: 'What makes our loneliness an anguish is not that I have no one to share my burden, but this: I have only my own burden to bear.' 'Loneliness is not a curse, but a blessing. It is the very tool that helps us discover who we are and what path to follow – the purpose of loneliness is nothing more than a call for action' (Chuck Gallozzi).

✛ HELPING OTHERS

With this in mind, there are many helpful suggestions that may help stem the degree of loneliness people often feel at this time of year. From the point of view of the outsider, it is important to take a sensitive approach. Patiently try to discover how those alone would like to spend the holiday – be it the day of Christmas or the few days leading up to and following it. Maybe the family home is not the place for everyone. Maybe it is too suffocating, maybe it imposes too much strained bonhomie. Try to ascertain if there is a way people's needs can be met – a certain degree of compromise is necessary. It should be remembered that Christmas is a season rather than just one day; the important thing is not that the entire family is together in the family home, but that the individual family members are happy, safe and healthy. Freeing oneself from the 'traditional family Christmas' might indeed be quite liberating. Indeed, as we discovered in the previous chapter, at the traditional Irish Christmas Day festival many people might really prefer to be elsewhere. All this does go to show how alternative arrangements can be made to ensure that those who might otherwise be alone on Christmas day (or during the season) might be included in the magic of God's glory and the mystery of Christ's birth.

If it is inevitable that you will be spending time alone during Christmas, it is a good idea to look into volunteering for local charities or shelters. Often, people do devote their Christmas Day to serving the homeless, and many community halls are festively decorated and festooned with all the paraphernalia of Christmas in order to bring cheer to the lives of not just those without homes, but those who are maybe old or sickly, thus making the day a bit more tolerable, a bit more joyful. (It is important to remember those elderly in our own families that may have been forgotten.) Even though it might be the last thing one feels like doing, the somewhat selfish benefits of having felt like the day has been an accomplishment and a comfort to others make it worthwhile.

Spending time alone needn't be such a chore. Some people find it beneficial to get out into nature and celebrate the birth and glory of Christ by celebrating the wonder and beauty of his creation. Many activities are organised to such an end. One such is the annual Goal Mile, which takes place in fifty-two places around Ireland, such as UCD, Dublin and NUIG, Galway (see www.Goal.ie for further details). This could then be expanded out into meeting with those on the morning of such activities, sharing a leisurely breakfast or organising an evening meal in a willing participant's house.

The spirit of community often comes into play when extending the spirit of Christmas. Knowing our neighbours, knowing where they're coming from and some of the difficulties they can face might also lead to a chance encounter with a lonely soul over the period of Christmas. Even just being aware of the fact that others are alone for Christmas, recognising this and extending an invite might be all the acknowledgement those alone for Christmas need. Often people are embarrassed to ask for some company on Christmas Day, perhaps embarrassed to find themselves in such an isolated situation. We should be aware that an outstretched hand is all one needs to lessen the emotional burden that is often part of the Christmas season.

This is especially true of elderly neighbours, who often find the day goes without so much as a phone call. It does not require much community spirit to take into account those who might be living alone, with family far away or perhaps with no family at all, yet it means so much to those in such isolated situations.

This is equally true of people who unfortunately have to spend the season in hospital. While such stays are difficult at the best of times, Christmas day and the forced festive cheer can often take much more of an emotional toll. Why not organise a troupe of Christmas carollers to bring some musical (and perhaps comic!) entertainment to such patients? Even stopping to talk to some of those stuck in hospital, should we be in visiting a relative or friend, can make the world of difference. The same often applies to those living in nursing homes. Often it is the case that they have no family close by, or indeed no family at all. This can be a very lonely experience. Just a few minutes taken to acknowledge such a situation by exchanging a few words is often all it takes to brighten someone's day. Indeed it can prove uplifting for both parties.

Alternatively, if we are in a position to do so, perhaps we should take the initiative to organise a Christmas meal for friends and acquaintances that may be in a similar situation to us. Those separated from family can in this way find a different type of family with which to celebrate the day.

✛ HELPING OURSELVES

For those who have been bereaved in the recent year, or indeed at any time, of a spouse, sibling, parent or partner, Christmas proves a very melancholic and lonely time. Not only do we not feel like socialising or entertaining, we often feel guilty for even harbouring such thoughts of merriment. It then proves important to remind ourselves that there is no need to feel guilty, indeed no point to it. We must be allowed to feel sad. Christmas might then be seen as a way to reflect on the past year, to remember loved ones now gone in a special way. It is important at such a time to consider organising ways of getting out of the house or away from the traditional family set-up, as it once might have been. Christmas dinner in a hotel a few days out of the country might be beneficial in breaking the familiarity as it once was. It is important in such a situation that we have some family or close friends around to provide emotional back-up.

Because of the forced merriment that Christmas often entails, it is not surprising that people who may not even be without family or friends with which to celebrate it often find themselves depressed and alone. Again, feelings of guilt and of being unappreciative often creep in. Remember, it is entirely normal to feel like this. Also remember that it is up to us to drag ourselves out of such an emotional mire. Acknowledging feelings of loneliness and down-heartedness and then getting on with the day at hand is often the best way of getting through the Christmas season.

In summary, Christmas can be a lonely time for many for a variety of reasons. Whether it's the first one away from home, the first since the death of a loved one or just another in a line of many isolated from family and friends, we all need to be aware of what we can do for others and for ourselves in such situations.

✛ TIPS

- Ascertaining what it is we think others might appreciate and enjoy the most on Christmas day can help curb feelings of isolation and loneliness.

- Getting out of the house, volunteering, being active, all promote a more healthy attitude to the day.

- Becoming acquainted with our neighbours, especially our elderly neighbours, and taking into account their needs for the day could go a long way to spreading the festive cheer.

- Paying a visit to those stuck in hospital or living in a nursing home can prove beneficial not just to those visited but to those doing the visiting.

- Acknowledging feelings of grievance and reflecting on the lives of loved ones now gone, accompanied by family or supportive friends, can make something positive out of an often sad and melancholic time.

✛ PRAYER

Lord, when loneliness closes in, help me
to take comfort that you are with me.
In my darkest hours, deliver me from my
fears and worries, as you delivered your
servant Job.
Let me be guided by the Christmas child
who came to banish the night forever.
Help me to trust in the promise of
Christmas peace and to share it with
those I meet today.

Resources

ACCORD

Central Office
Columba Centre
Maynooth
Co Kildare
Tel: 01 505 3112
Fax: 01 601 6410
Email: admin@accord.ie
Web: www.accord.ie

BÓTHAR

Head Office
Old Clare Street
FREEPOST
Limerick
Tel: 061 414142
Fax: 061 315833
Freephone: 1800 268 463

Northern Ireland Freephone: 0800 039 0267
Email: info@bothar.ie
Web: www.bothar.org

FINANCIAL REGULATOR

Consumer Information Department
Financial Regulator
P.O. Box 9138
College Green
Dublin 2
Lo-call: 1980 200 469
Email: consumerinfo@financialregulator.ie
Web: www.itsyourmoney.ie

GINGERBREAD IRELAND

Carmichael House
North Brunswick Street
Dublin 7
Tel: 01 814 6618
Fax: 01 814 6619
Email: info@gingerbread.ie
Web: www.gingerbread.ie

GOAL IRELAND

12 Cumberland Street
Dun Laoghaire
Co. Dublin
Tel: 01 280 9779
Fax: 01 280 9215
Email: info@goal.ie
Web: www.goal.ie

TRÓCAIRE

Maynooth
Co. Kildare
Callsave (RoI): 1850 408 408
Freephone (Northern Ireland): 0800 912 1200
Email: info@trocaire.ie
Web: www.trocaire.org

Acknowledgements

Extract from *Waiting in Hope* (p. 10), by Tony Flannery, Veritas, 2002.

Lines from Patrick Kavanagh's 'Advent' (p. 12), taken from *Collected Poems*, Antoinette Quinn (ed.), Allen Lane, 2007; by kind permission of the Trustees of the Estate of the late Katherine B. Kavanagh, through the Jonathan Williams Literary Agency.

Lines from Robert Graves' 'Hedges Freaked with Snow' (p. 39), taken from *Explorations 1*, Gill and Macmillan, 1985.

Extracts from *Design for Wholeness: Dealing with Anger, Learning to Forgive, Building Self-Esteem* (pp. 49–50), by Loughlan Sofield, Carroll Juliano and Rosine Hammett, Ave Maria Press, 1990.

Extract from *Amongst Women* (p. 61) by John McGahern, Penguin, 1991.

Lines from Gerard Manley Hopkin's Sonnet 65, 'No worst, there is none' (p. 72), taken from *Poems of Gerard Manley Hopkins*, Robert Bridges (ed.), Kessinger Publishing, 2004.

Lines from Robert Frost's 'Acquainted with the Night' (p. 73), taken from *New Hampshire*, Holt Publications, 1923.